Visual Signals

Issue zero

JUNE-JULY 2020 ISSUE

Introduction

What's up my future friends?! This is KITE0080 of Musics the Hang Up. For the longest time I've wanted to put out some sort of monthly physical. I really wanted to cement my style and creativity in the scene before producing one but I always worried about interfering with Private Suite Magazine (Arguably the best Vaporwave magazine). So I released the *Book of Visual Signalwave*. I've some how hit a niche in publishing that as I have almost sold over 500 copies of the book! Thank every single one of you who has help me reach that number. You guys are amazing. Oddly enough more that 80% of you are from Japan. あ りがとうございました~

I've always tried keeping my personal life out of my Youtube videos and Twitter/Instagram posts. So it might come as a shock to find out that I've been working on MTHU full time since April of 2019. I've been without a job since then, working on various projects from cassette releases, books, videos, album reviews, artist interviews, weird programmatically made albums, updating the website and so much more. It's been a hell of an adventure but as of June 22nd, 2020, I've retreated back to the workforce. I couldn't figure out how to turn MTHU into an escape from the 9-5.

I am moving from North Carolina to San Francisco as I've been sleeping on my Dad's couch for 6 months. Unfortunately, Covid-19 hit me harder than I expect as I lost my apartment in China and resorted to being stuck in my boring hometown. I've finally accepted my fate and found an amazing startup to focus my energy on.

Because of this, I don't think I'll be able to do MTHU the same way anymore. I would love for this irregular serial to be come out every month but my life is changing too much that I know I won't be able to do it justice.

So think of this little pocket-size, cheaply price publication as what's been in my mind during these last days of freedom; "my goodbye for a while" project. I will return and try to turn this project into what I dream it should be. Just give me time.

As always I want to thank my family, friends, fans and those who supported me for over a year. Without you I wouldn't have made traveled the world meeting you and dancing to Future Funk and Vaporwave together. I wouldn't have made over 50 podcast episodes. I wouldn't have made almost 100 Youtube videos. I wouldn't have collaborated with Pad or Private Suite or even worked on the *Nobody Here* Documentary. Until then, I'll keep the website (musicsthehangup.com) up to date with vapor releases and will always be on Discord. Feel free to reach out. I hope you enjoy this book~

Cheers,
KITE0080

Patreon "温" Crew
Chiefahleaf
Com_Zepol
Darkfez Futuretro
Middle Class Comfort
Groovy Kaiju
N3kkun
Q
Shadab Hassan
THOR MAILLET
Vayu
Yoshcko

Follow This Project on Twitter:
@SignalsVisual

Track Reviews

Cursebreaker x theme - Equip

Vaporwave traditionally conforms to cityscapes and malls. Equip escapes from those realms and brings us into the world of fantasy. Fans of Castlevania and Final Fantasy will find plenty of enjoyment in Equip's video game sounding world. This theme says it all, you know you're in for an adventure.

Surfin' - I Kno

An album and artist that has been under the shadows for too long. In the track *Surfin'*, I Kno uses complex chopping and fast paced beats to keep the grooves strong and is ready to be in more live sets. Don't sleep on this one.

Two Of Us - Night Tempo

The prince of City pop took a chance and explored musics outside of japan with Bill Withers; an amazing jazz artist. Sampling is smooth, vocals hit the high points and the City pop twist stands out own its own. Night Tempo delivers again~

ドリーミング - Crystal Cola

After hour vibes in an anime landscape of teenage love and unpredictable adventure. A mix of Synthwave and City pop.

DESTINE - VECTOR GRAPHICS

A classic from the early days when vaporwave didn't care about music structure. This track starts with groovy bass-lines, transitions to chirpy bells and finally ends with catchy vocal sampling. VECTOR GRAPHICS is an OG with this 2015 release.

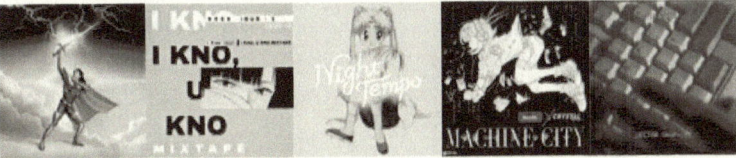

Free Drum Patterns

Every once in a while I hear something interesting in a song or just want to break away from my normal drum loops. Below are some interesting drum arrangements I've been messing with.

Basic House (120 BPM)

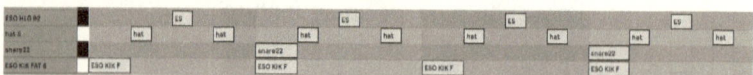

EDM Beat 1 (125 BPM)

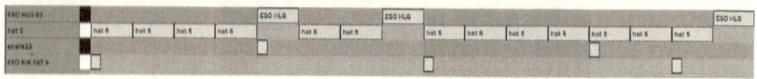

Trap Build Up (135 BPM)

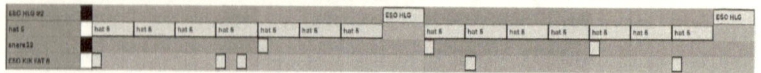

Jungle-ish (150 BPM)

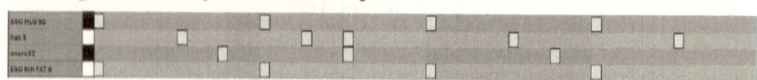

Suicide Boys Drums (125 BPM)

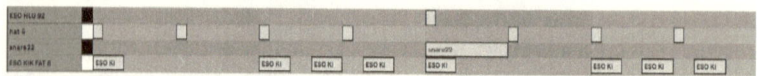

It's always interesting to play with triplets or stack a snare and bass for an added effect. Mess with the velocities or time signatures to see what works best for you. Let me know on Twitter if you use any of these in a track, I'd love to listen to it.

Digital artist spotlight

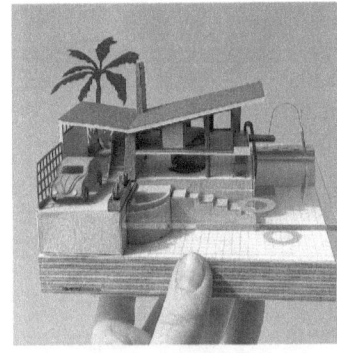

Ellie Sampson (London) uses paper, wood and minimal amount of material to design dreamy architectural models.

Often times, she finds real locations and models them in her own lo-fi paper aesthetic as intimate scenes. I love how she is precise with when to add details and when to use solid long sheets.

In this recreation of *Rona Road*, her crafting table and the view outside her presumed window has perfect purpose. The focus outside the window enforces this idea by not fully using her computer screen and fitting her workspace to the width of the actual window. It's a little slice of her life, without including the other aspects of her room that doesn't serve the purpose of what she wants the viewer to feel and see.

These are wonderful scenes to experience. I hope you find as much enjoyment in these scene as I do.

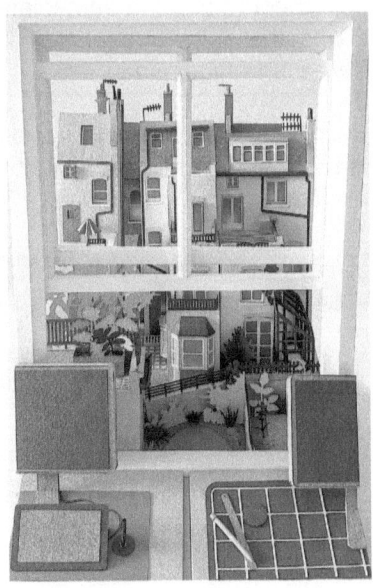

Find her on Twitter and Instagram @elliejsampson

HATENA – Parader (Review)

Hatena's album Parader is one of my favorite albums from this genre without question. I first heard it on Hatena's personal Bandcamp page and later picked up the cassette (a few copies left as of this writing, go get one!) on Coraspect's Bandcamp page. The digital version and cassette version are mixed differently and really makes the cassette feel that much more special. I can't wait to see what Hatena produces next or if this will come on wax any time soon.

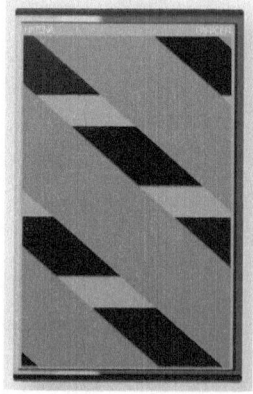

The perfectly timed cuts and seamless chopping are what I live for and Hatena has mastered that in more ways than one cementing this album as a classic. A few songs come to mind immediately on this album that really show cases the skills and effects I love in this genre: *365*, *Cheap Thrills*, and *Right Now*.

Even though Hatena may not be a big fan of this album himself, it is by far one of my top 5 of all time albums of Future Funk and it plays almost daily in my car. — N3KKUN

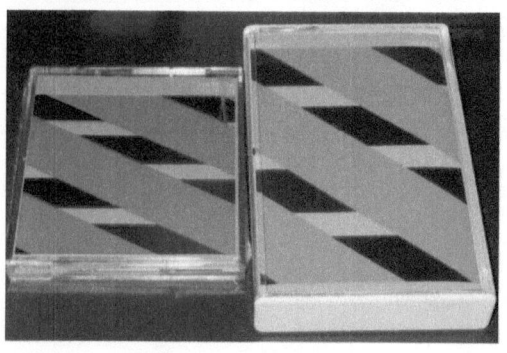

(left) N3KKUN's personal collection of the album

Label Talk With Zico

How did you get into Vaporwave?

- The start of it seemed rather bizarre, but I encountered Macintosh Plus' *Lisa Frank 420* when it became a meme back in the summer of 2016. Despite a chuckle and a pass on, I decided to look into it, and discovered more than just that; Saint Pepsi's *Enjoy Yourself*, Macross 82-99's "Fun Tonight", and Yung Bae's *Bae City Rollaz*. But my obsession didn't grow much until summer of 2018 in which I found myself into the realms of Artzie Music, their latest uploads, and even watching the top anime that they feature (Urusei Yatsura).

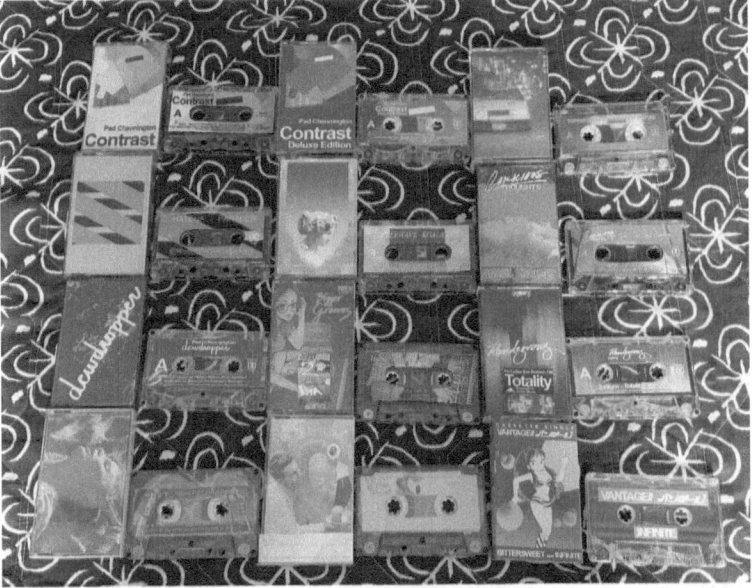

Before FCC, were you already dubbing home-made cassettes?

- I started my cassette obsession back in January 2018 when I bought a cheap shoebox cassette recorder and blank tapes; All I ever did is record meme songs onto tape and make watered down mixtapes. I even took to photoshop to make the j-card.

Then, it came to a rise when a classmate offered me blank tapes, and I bought a mid-range Sanyo cassette deck. And so, I've been making my homedubs throughout the summer of 2018, and looking up auctions for New Old Stock tapes.

What kind of tech do you use to home dub for your label?
- At first, I just found whatever I can find around the house; a computer, a generic HP Printer, photo paper, and a cassette deck that I can use, along with tapes I can dub. Overtime, I have upgraded those when it started to kick off along with seeking advice from other labels, from making my printing and cutting jobs better, to full on replacing things and making them better. I have recently upgraded to a new EPSON printer in which it does a better job than before, and I am also investing in a high end cassette deck, especially when I want the cassette to give some definition like it came fresh from the factory, all with DIY's glory. All the while, I have been using an old iPhone playing a single wav file of Side A and B, but after seeking advice, I would rather veer to a Digital to Analog Converter, which would bring out the analog sound to digital files.

What advice do you have for new in-house cassette labels?
- It is best to start off just-for-kicks or for keeps. That way, you will see how the hobby goes. And if you are truly dedicated to that, it is best to take everything that is wrong about it (in the customer's shoes) and get rid of it. Once that is done, it is best to take everything that was good about it and make it better. I highly recommend taking some advice as well; other labels in this scene in my eyes aren't really competitors, and so they might be willing to help out on how a label should be run.

What's the big dream for First Class Collective?
- My big dream for First Class Collective is to live up to the big artists in the game; release some iconic albums, and still keep in touch and give a leg up with the small ones. We are already starting to have releases to go by leaps and bounds, heck we have a vinyl release coming soon!

...Read the full Interview on musicsthehangup.com

Now Available On Amazon!

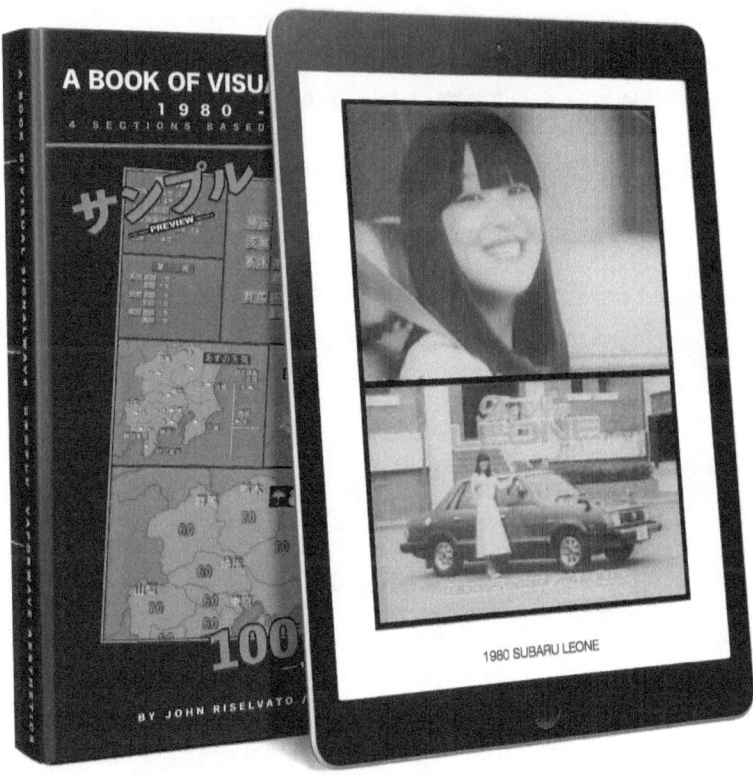

1980 SUBARU LEONE

"A Book of Visual Signalwave" is the experience, feels and emotions found in Japanese television from the years 1980 to 2001. The world of Signalwave and its music has always had a visual side. This book is a contribution to the music genre in a different way with a focus on a period of time, the commercials, tv and cars. This book is pure Signalwave for the eyes! Over over 90 pages of commercials turned into comic book form. Each commercial should be viewed as an individual art piece that evokes emotional ties felt in Vaporwave.

Available in Paperback and Kindle

Scene news

RIP 2004アメリカンイーグルポロ

It was announced earlier in the June on Reddit that Bobby AKA 2004アメリカンイーグルポロ has unfortunately passed away. I personally didn't know him but the community came together to celebrate his life and share their experiences with him. We saw how our good friend, Vayu, released his cassette, *Voidworld*. How earlier in the month, Vapor Memory did a stream in his memory and for once the Reddit community came together to be respectful of the situation.

It's always sad to lose a member of our community, especially at the age of 23. u/TheBraveToast didn't give us much information about the death but he did write:

> "I will remember him for his love of dogs, obscure memes, making fun of stupid stuff on the internet, generally strange content, designer clothing, flashy watches, poor taste comedy, and getting stoned with his buddies. He was a strange and generous soul, a truly odd and good egg."

RIP 2004アメリカンイーグルポロ, thank you for creating such beautiful vaporwave. Your legacy will always live on in our scene. If anyone has any stories they wish to share with the community about him, please join the discussion on Reddit. It'll be a nice way for future generations who find his music to discover him.

Listen to the *Voidworld* on Wave Racer Collective:
https://waveracerscollective.bandcamp.com/album/voidworld

Help Nmesh Find his stolen car!

Although not specific to the scene, the crazy events behind Nmesh accidentally leaving his car keys in the ignition and getting caught up in a gas station, leading into a high-speed chase has to be documented. "a guy at [the] opposite end of the pumps screams out his car window 'they got your car!! get in!!!' - I don't know this guy, but what the fuck else am I supposed to do?" Nmesh stated on Instagram. After white-knuckling a clip from fast & furious the police take over and unfortunately, the criminals

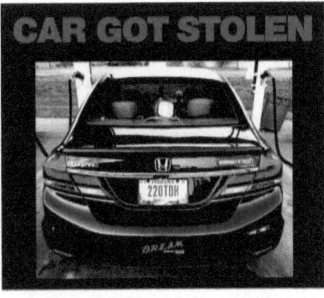

getaway. 2 days later, the car returned to NMESH but the criminals completely trashed the car.

"fuckers trashed my car and stole everything out of it - etched a giant "H" onto the hood - removed all my stickers - took Lucy's car seat - guessing they blew a tire while they were driving like assholes, cos the spare is on - burnholes on the floor mat. they left a phone tho"

What a strange turn of events. Sucks the car got returned in such horrible condition but happy ending? I guess... Oddly enough, they tried removing the Nmesh sticker off the bumper but without avail. Nmesh lives on~

Aloe City Records gets a DMCA

It seems every few weeks someone has had enough with their experience with Tracking Waves and turns to social media to warn everyone not to buy from them. Countless members of the community eventually have enough of the silence from the label when months pass without receiving their cassettes they paid for. This time around people started complaining about not getting

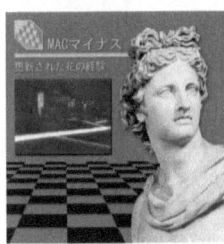

their Updated Floral Experience by MACマイ ナス cassette, and ACR took it upon themselves to release the cassette on their label and fundraise enough money to give free copies away to those who lost their money from Tracking Waves scam.

It was amazing to see a label step up and take control of the situation and help out those who just want their cassettes. The funding was going well but then all of a sudden, the label got an email from Bandcamp for a take down request.

Tracking Waves would rather spend their time sending out DMCAs instead of just shipping their cassettes. It's a sad state of the scene and it sucks people are getting suckered into their labels lies. I just want to add, thank Aloe City Records for being the bigger label. Everyone stay away from Tracking Waves. You're just going to lose your money. I've lost out on two cassettes myself. I've learned my lesson. Let's hope this is will help inform future fans.

Got news?
Did we miss any news or have something to announce for next month? Send us an email at contact@musicsthehangup.com

Concerts

猫 シ Corp plays an ambient show
"First 25 minutes is 猫 シ Corp. ! I did an ambient set live with old and also new unreleased material..." - 猫 シ Corp

Watch here: https://bit.ly/2YC1kxc

Pad Chennington's Block Party (PCBP)
PCBP was an all day even with two stages featuring 26 different artists. Leading up to June 20th, Pad had a special guests streaming random events like playing video games or doing fan interviews. Pad's own label, KATS KILL RECORDS, ran the "Upper Cut" stages, while VAPOR MEMORY ran the "Southpaw Stage". This event was dedicated to the memory of George Floyd and his family, and was use to donate to his Memorial Fund. It was amazing to see ev.exi, Tsudio Studio, HATENA, Ahero, Shoji and PowerPCME.

Pad is uploading each set on his labels YouTube channel but at the moment it seems its replay is limited.

Most artists are uploading their own sets to their own YouTube and Patron channels. Find more information from the respective artist.

Congrats Pad for putting together such a massive event. It turned out better than I think people expected. It'll do down in the history books as it was probably the biggest concert of the summer. I just wish it was going on every weekend — KITE0080

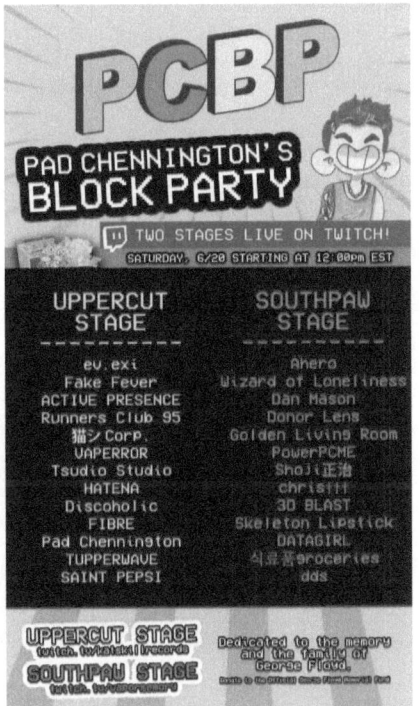

VIRTUAL MEMORY 11

Pacific Plaza Records (@PacificPlazaRec) held another digital concert featuring Augnos, Phantacat and Yung Shiro. Stating, "All money raised will be split between The Peoples City Council LA and The Okra Project."

Interestingly enough, they had an RSVP on Facebook which I thought was a really good idea to remind people of the show and to get other people interested considering it was hosted on Twitch. URL Parties are really becoming big news in through these "strange times" of covid-19. Glad people are still interested in listening to good music live.
— KITE0080

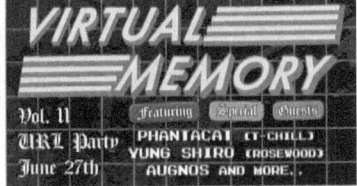

New & Noteworthy

Voidworld by 2004アメリカンイーグルポロ

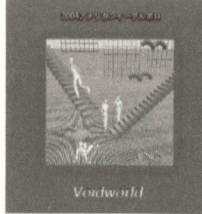

Voidworld, a dark empty world with melodic additions the further you explore it. From being welcomed into the OS to shutting down, this album is full of dreamscapes and simulation vibes that will always stand the test of time. Let's keep his legacy alive by taking a listen every once in a while. Favorite Track: *Psychedelic Breeze*

Return 2 The Source - Feat Jensen Interceptor & SHED by DJ Haus

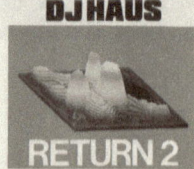

This 5 track album encompasses what I imagined minimalism in dance would sound like; *Primitive frequencies* mixed with high action percussion. Oftentimes the track might seem too minimal but with the right set of headphones, a layer of complexity can be found. It makes for the experience of listen to the album more of a hunt of music in the chaos instead of music in itself. Favorite Track: *Bit Too Deep (SHED Remix)*

Sentimental Transmission by 天気予報

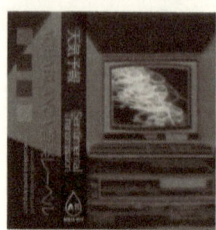

I recently bought this on cassette after Siobhan (on discord) told me it was one of their favorite 天気予報 albums. They described it was an album that always made them tear up a little and I totally agree. There's something more sorrowful inside and I think it's because of the crackling vinyl on every track. Additionally, the first track on the album sets the mood better than any other album of 天気予報. The reverb on the peaceful piano and the static brings back past memories and hopefulness. It actually reminds me of a specific street outside my old apartment in 八卦嶺. A street where the sun once rose over the Japanese named hotel. The cross section between my apartment and the construction in front of the my second favorite pizza place. The long streets I used to ride a bike to work on. The few times I would ride my skateboard to Starbucks to read a book. Those moments I'll never get back. Those memories are my own sentimental transmissions. Favorite Track: Crumbling

Bonemann Radio by Bonemann

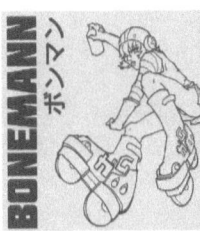

This isn't your typical vapor release as it plays off the idea of piracy and plunderphonics to make complex and groovy mashups. Each track takes elements from late pop culture and turns them into new experiences. It's different than hip-hop or DJing, but I can see it's roots. Favorite Track: What A Rush (open up for Dave, already!)

Clairvoyance by Monokawa

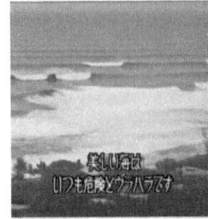

A beautiful collection of ambient plunderphonics ripped straight from the artists late grandfather's vinyl collection. Each track has an eerie tone and amplified cracks to really set the mood. The sample selected is incredible and It's nice their grandpa can live on in the digital realms. Favorite Track: It May Look Peaceful, But Danger is Always Present

不是你的春夢 Not Your Wet Dream by 我是機車少女 i'mdifficult

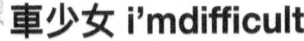
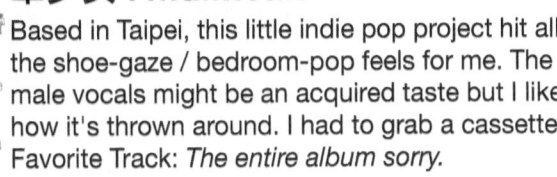

Based in Taipei, this little indie pop project hit all the shoe-gaze / bedroom-pop feels for me. The male vocals might be an acquired taste but I like how it's thrown around. I had to grab a cassette. Favorite Track: *The entire album sorry.*

Top Releases of June

1. Mannequin Challenge by GOOD NEWS (bottom)
2. 1985 by haircuts for men

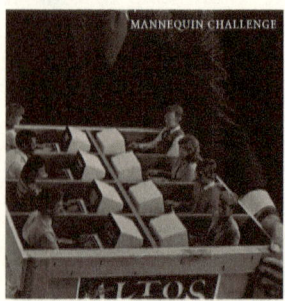

3. I Love Hating You by FrankJavCee
4. BLESS ME / 裸のSummer by オリーブがある
5. Afterglow by bl00dwave
6. Seele EP by Computer Data
7. Nah... by Nah…
8. ждите Нас Звезды! by Project Lazarus
9. HAWAII MADISON by AIRMAX
10. slowdance,lowtide by Hirotaka Shirotsubaki
11. 常夏 by desert sand feels warm at night
12. NOBODY HERE: The Story Of Vaporwave by Various Artists
13. George Clanton & Nick Hexum by George Clanton & Nick Hexum
14. VHS CAMERA by machina pensant
15. Virtual Loneliness by ll nøthing ll
16. AVlandia by AV 0
17. House Plants by Jomero
18. Gardens by Dirty Art Club (right)
19. SYSTEM OVERRIDE by AceMo
20. Zeroin by Dope Smoker
21. hybtwibt? by Space Afrika
22. Stax Trax by Candid Trax

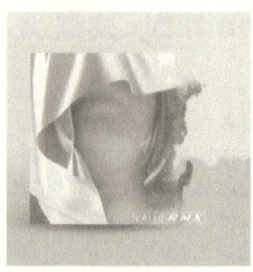

23. The House EP by Vhahn
24. VA:10.RMX by Various Artists (left)
25. Bonemann Radio by Bonemann
26. 「 kimi no machi 」君の街 ビクター M K I I
27. Dungeon Explorer by スーパー1999コンソール (Digital)

Find more on: musicsthehangup.com/

SONY ICF-SW100 SW Radio

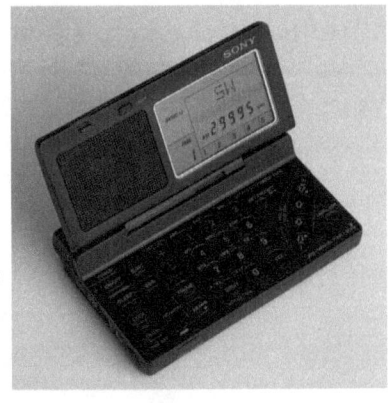

Year Introduced: *1994*
Power: *Battery (2 AA) & external mains adaptor*
Size: *155 x 90 x 33 mm*
Weight: *240 g*
Coverage: *150 kHz - 30 MHz, FM (stereo on headphones)*

Every once in a while I surf through eBay looking for retro technology of yesteryear. Earlier in the month I stumbled into the world of shortwave radios after years of being away from the scene. I remember in earl 2010s I was super into shortwave and even reached out to my local Linux User Group seeing if anyone wanted to start a SW Radio club. It didn't turn into anything but I did buy a couple of

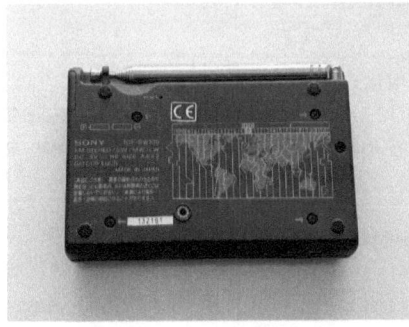

shortwave radios, listened to a few foreign country broadcasts and found it interesting but not something I stuck with in the long term.

Regardless of my story, I found this specific Sony SW Radio aesthetically pleasing. In a lot of ways it reminds me of an early slider phone mixed with a flip phone but here, the keyboard on the bottom half is used to punch in frequencies. You can listen to FM and AM radio as well as Shortwave. The speaker next to the display fits perfectly in the top. On the back it has a world map with UTC timezones. It's wonderful. I didn't buy it but I still admire the design. Sony wins again with winning me over as a fan of their craft. —KITE0080

NATIONALナショナル interview

MTHU had a chance to sit down with Malaysian Future Funk artist, NATIONAL ナショナル, for a quick interview about their Vapor Career. NATIONAL ナショナル has been in the Future Funk scene since Sept, 2016, releasing dozens of EP/singles and albums and as of recently on cassette with First Class Collective. They are on top of their game and I had to learn more about them. Follow NATIONAL ナショナル on Twitter: @FM_NATIONAL_

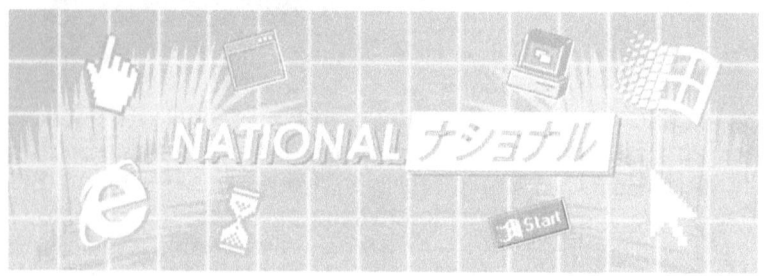

How did you get into future funk?
- Through Youtube recommended section. A music video called "Saint Pepsi - Tell me". I've constantly played the song for a week.

You've released multiple cassettes, when can we expect a vinyl release?
- Maybe? I tried to do a vinyl release on Qrates but I don't have the minimum required backers to fund the release. It got like 34/100 backers. The number of audiences is not there yet.

Who are your biggest influences?
- Tendencies, Unibe@t, Cape Coral, Childhood, Dante Mars Ajeto, Supersex420, CVLTVRΣ and S U R F I N G.

Who is your favorite label you've worked with?
- First Class Collective.

Do you have any interesting Future Funk stories (with other artists / label / fans)?
- That one time, I discovered another Malaysian making Future Funk music. He remixed old 80s malay disco songs. His music was featured on Artzie Music channel. The music video was called 'F i 7 i - Red is my fav colour too'. Then I realized there were only 2 people in Malaysia making future funk music (maybe). I think people don't know future funk or vaporwave because it is not a very popular genre here.

How would you describe the N A T I O N A L ナショナル Aesthetic?
- Pastel colours, old 80s 90s computers, Windows XP 95, palm trees, tropical flowers, Kuala Lumpur city.

If you had to pick one song to introduce NATIONAL ナショナル to new fans, what song would it be?
- 【T R O P I C A L】// ゴニが

What does 2020 look like for NATIONAL ナショナル?
- Mixed. Released two songs and an album on cassette. The First Class Collective label did a great job. I stayed in my room everyday because of the outbreak. So, I got nothing to do but play games, especially Minecraft. I thought I could advertise and expose them to future funk and vaporwave.

Find NATIONAL ナショナル on Bandcamp:
https://fmnational.bandcamp.com

New Vaporwave Documentary!

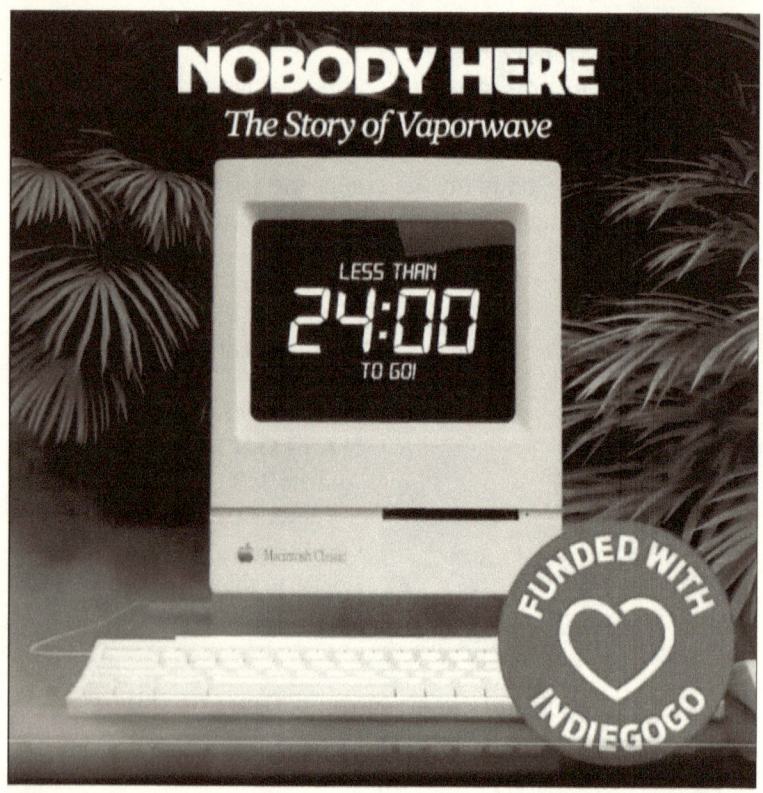

I've been working on the *Nobody Here: The Story of Vaporwave* documentary for a couple months now. I'm happy to announce the Indiegogo campaign was fully funded and we started reaching out and interviewing top artists in the scene. Things are rather hush hush right now but it's going to be huge! The MyPetFlamingo guys plus the support team are doing amazing work to make a vaporwave documentary everyone expects and deserves in this scene. To stay up to date on the project follow the twitter @NobodyHere_Film

Tatsuro Yamashita – Melodies

City pop (シティーポップ) legend Tatsuro Yamashita releases album Melodies on Moon Records on this month (June) in 1983. This jazzy, funk and soul pop Japanese album comprised of 10 tracks with the track Marry-go-Round (メリー・ゴー・ラウンド) being the most popular. The pure sounds of this track's bass line and his vocals are a direct reflection of that Japanese 80 vibe we've all come to love.

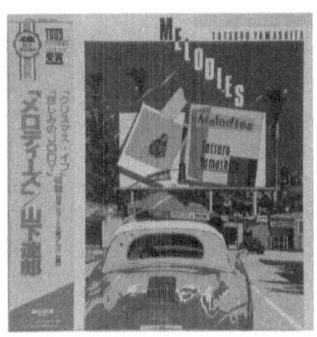

There were various releases on cassette, vinyl and even had a 30th anniversary release a couple years back. It's a staple for the genre and has stood the test of time.

The full album can be found on Youtube and there are plenty of physical versions for purchase on Discogs.

Romaji titles / Japanese titles:

A1: Kanashimi no Jody (She Was Crying) / 悲しみのJody

A2: Koukiatsu Girl / 高気圧ガール

A3: Yashou (Night-Fly) / 夜翔 (Night-Fly)

A4: Guess I'm Dumb

A5: Hitotoki / ひととき

B1: Merry-Go-Round / メリー・ゴー・ラウンド

B2: Blue Midnight

B3: Ashioto / あしおと

B4: Mokusou / 黙想

B5: Christmas Eve / クリスマス・イブ

ジェイディーエム Dealership

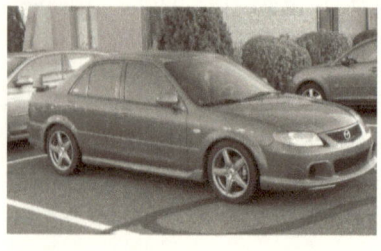

Mazda Protege 2003, Blue racing race seats, no back seats. 95,230 miles. A joy to drive. One owner from new. Only served at main dealers. Always meticulously looked after. Bodywork is in perfect condition. runs and stops perfectly. Electronic windows. 19-inch alloy rims + spare. $8,500 USD.

Subaru STi WRX 2001, bug-eye. Subaru blue with custom pink STi emblem. Custom front splitter. Full tinted windows. Matte black 20-inch rims. Lowered. COBB access-port. IHI VG52 Turbo. Kenwood system. Spec-D blue tip exhaust. Perfect paint. No rust. Look for $10,500

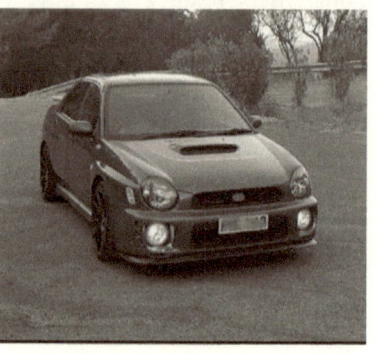

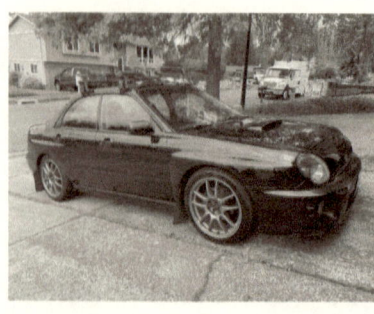

Subaru Impreza 2.5 RS 2002, clean title. 3rd owner. New spark plugs and timing belt. Clutch is mint. Yakima Roof rack. WRX hood and interior seats. 5 speed. Oil changes done on time. All 4 OEM tires. just hit 200k Miles and runs like a champ. Lowered on WRX spring. Sounds like a WRX. Amazing in the snow. asking $5.5k, no low balling.

Upcoming releases

Below are some upcoming releases announced publicly on Twitter. Quoted exactly from the artist or label:

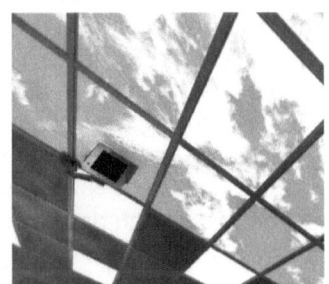

- "Donor Lens album 2, vinyl/cassette/MiniDisc/digital/mystery bonus format out on @MyPetFlamingoUK 31st July" - Donor Lens // @Donor_Lens (right)
- "Sleep District album coming out July 3rd. Chill wave/lofi hip hop vibes with vapor wave textures. Limited vinyl releases too" - Sweeps // @sweepsbeats
- "SPIRIT is coming to vinyl on the 3rd!! https://ahero.facewayrecords.com/album/spirit" - Ahero // @aherointl
- "I'm releasing an album! (life vest located under sea)" - VK // @VaporKitteh
- Hawaii94 Visualise is coming out July 10th on Subsubmarinee - Hawaii94 // @yoler0y
- "I want to release album in this month, with some gaming themes. Called "Press Start". I also have alternative versions of cover art" - Georgi1802 // @georgi1802
- "Yep! Got a WIP or two in the works - undecided which to drop so far, but likely you'll hear "Jomanda" get a release in July." - Strawberry Station // @StrawberryStat1
- "Im releasing another little noise bit called FL-GCoM FIELD LODGE RECORDINGS VOLUME 5. Интимный разговор" - Campcerous // @Scions8
- "well, there are two albums that possibly go in july. one is a original album, no samples. other one is going to be a mixtape,a apocalyptic version of pop music. here are the two covers of these upcoming albums" - ChiM.θ◀ريال ﷺ ﴿ بِسْــــــــمِ اللَّهِ الرَّحْمَنِ الرَّحِيمِ ﴾ // @Waterfall2117

- "Vylter (つ◕◡◕)つ ♥ what are you ♥ Coming to @VBCvaporwave vbc July 24th" - Vylter // @vylter
- "Re-releasing my Sleeparalysis Dreamchamber 3 album on @aquaoscura with bonus tracks and a physical release. Should be dropping late July" - SLEEPARALYSIS| DREAMCHAMBER // @sleeparalysis
- "I've got a song that I'm thinking of releasing as a single since It didn't match my current EP that I was working on, I'm just hung up on art for it." - LCD Noir // @LCD_Noir
- "antennae EP by jankyswans, July 3rd, via http://jankyswans.bandcamp.com." - jankyswans // @jankyswans
- "@videoheadcleanr when is Humility dropping, add a comment with details so Kite can add it to the list!" - C o m p u S e r v e へようこそ // @c0mpus3rv3
  - VIDEOHEADCLEANER // @videoheadcleanr: "Jun 16 June 30th is the cut off date. The album will be out on July 1st"
- "I have a new album released in April that I am still promoting And I'm working on a new mixtape I HOPE to release in July." - PKSkyler // @PKSkyler

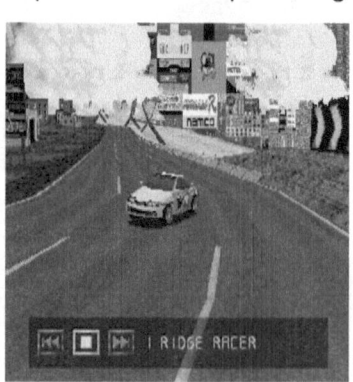

- "I have this project based on the first Ridge Racer dropping next month. It's a sort of follow up to the Tenchu beattape I released on the @Sunset_Grid sister label, GumShoe." - Shonen Sampler // @SamplerShonen

Thanks everyone who responded to Tweet asking for July releases. In future issues, I'll ask again and I hope we can build a massive release list for the next issue as well.

Did you listen to one of these releases? Go follow the artist on twitter and let them know~

Vaporwave Crossword

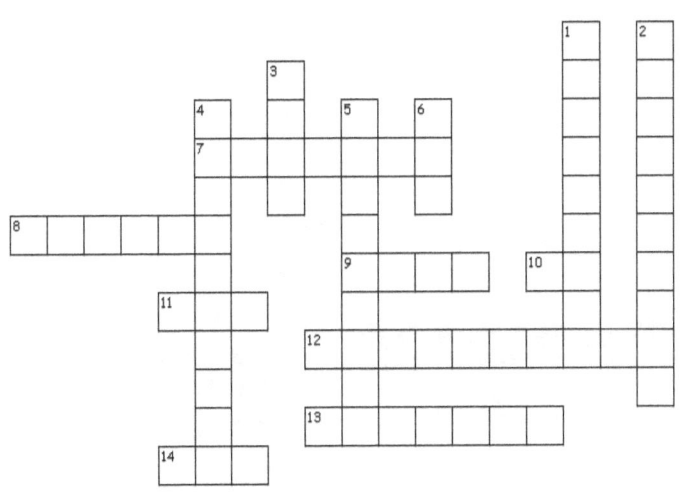

Across
7. folding paper
8. my favorite car
9. a type of gem
10. board game
11. zico plus MCC
12. yellow hair girl
13. average temperature
14. a game on this console

Down
1. my Japanese breakfast
2. music for anime girls
3. serial experiments
4. the real people inside
5. the best genre
6. baseball

* hint: most words can be found in this issue of Visual Signals

Bandcamp Label Starter Pack

internet label
starter package

 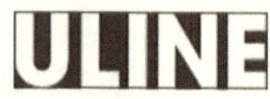

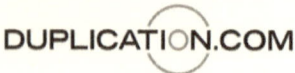 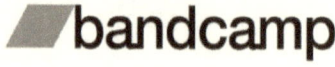

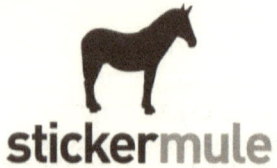

Status

Pre-Shipment

6 months

Get Updates ⌄

Credits: Q

Pokemon Ruby GameShark (GBA)

Master Code
A2E564FE
0FB58A54
530823D9
16558191

Legendary Pokemon

AERODACTYL
66582493 0FF88AD2
ARTICUNO
B8BABB07 1279065D
ZAPDOS
813E577F C64AB1BA
MOLTRES
5A8E3C77 1F661F0B
MEWTWO
649DA11D AC382E6A
MEW
13EAA696 65095035
RAIKOU
A10710E4 E472D0F8
ENTEI
5B01BDB2 183D8C74
SUICUNE
D25A4A77 A675F69A
LUGIA
4EECFE9F 27D82240
HO-OH
3D68FB8B 4B323185

CELEBI
ABAB4663 A9BDEC6F
REGIROCK
EE48CE33 DD9BA0C5
REGICE
B8E60141 9846F68D
REGISTEEL
79DFACFC CE3130F9
GROUDON
F655438D 3AA5C717
RAYQUAZA
F45F5684 50826322
LATIAS
9924490F 674355D7
LATIOS
B0EF6EE8 A714B8D9
JIRACHI
89CF0941 3F293D81
DEOXYS
88F7CB8E EE360350

Walkthrough walls
E03B0649 5D67050C
78DA95DF 44018CB4

Rare Candies in PC
280EA266 88A62E5C

Masterballs in PC
91B85743 27069397

インターネットイニシアティブ

日本語 ˅

お使いのインターネットの速度:

5.8 Mbps

詳細を表示

Need better internet in 2004? Move to Japan!
Accepting new Visa applications for qualified foreign friends.
Paid for by the 携帯電話 gang~

8-8-9-1-9 – ha-ya-ku-i-ku

("hurry up, let's go")

ぼくのなつやすみ (PSX)

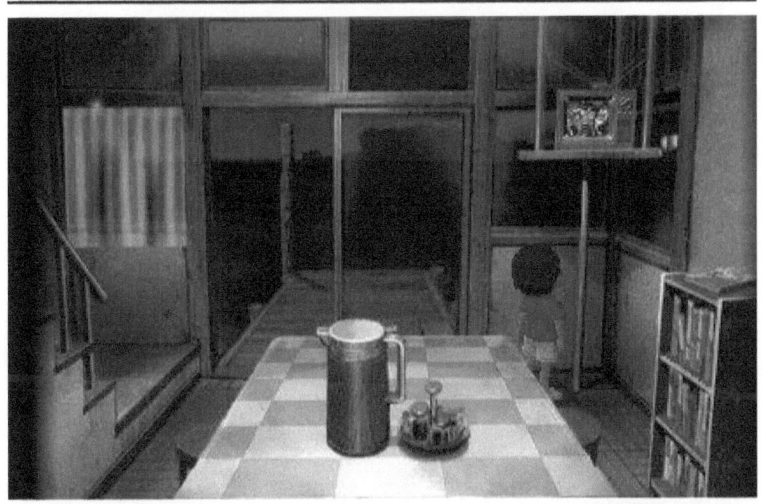

ぼくのなつやすみ or "My Summer Vacation" is a Japan slice of life video game through the eyes of a 9 year old boy. It's August 1975 and you have 31 days of summer vacation at your aunt and uncles wooded country side. Explore areas, catch bugs, collect bottle caps or fly a kite. It's the perfect summer holiday on the PSX (2000) or PSP (2006).

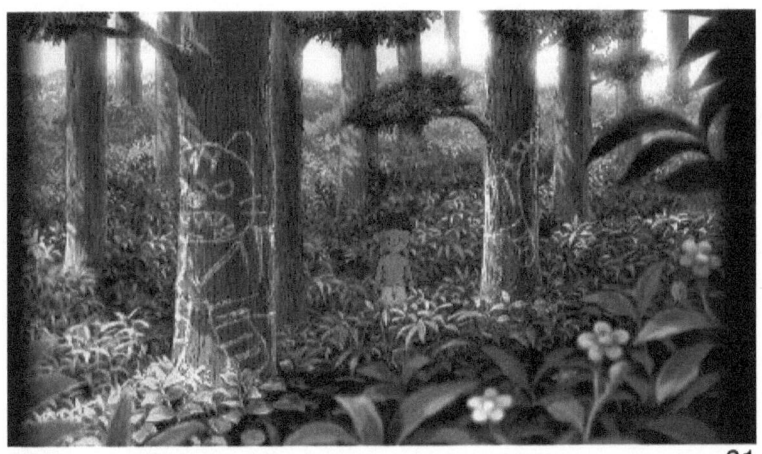

Recommended Manga

20th Century Boys

Based in 1969, 4 boys build a secret hideout to share manga and dirty mags while listening to radio. One of the boys draws a symbol in the base to signify their friendship. Before growing up, the "gang" dreams of a world in which the boys would fight against villains destroying their universe.

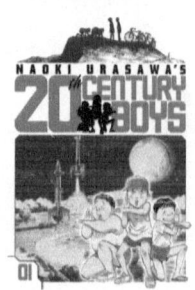

After 20+ years since their creation of various stories in their scenario book, their youthful imagination is starting to become reality. An amazing futuristic thriller series.

Homunculus

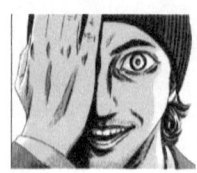

After the main character, Susumu Nakoshi, get's offered money for an experiment by an eccentric rich boy, he starts seeing homunculus figures in every day people. The hole in his forehead is either making him go crazy or he has the ability to see peoples true image. It's creepy, it's grotesque and probably one of the best page turners in manga. It made me fall in love with reading manga again.

Mix

Mix is a Japanese baseball themed shōnen that's actually a sequel to *Touch*. It's cool to see how some of the characters in the sequel have grown up and how the main character is following the footsteps of those who brought baseball into the limelight at their junior high-school. It kind of give me the same vibes as initial-d but for baseball.

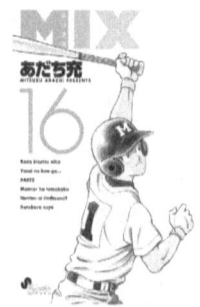

Learn Chinese - HSK 1

I've been learning Chinese for 3 years now. Everyone starts with HSK 1, here are 27 to get your introduced to the beautiful ancient language.

我	wǒ	I, me
我们	wǒmen	we, us (pl.)
你	nǐ	you
你们	nǐmen	you (pl.)
他	tā	he, him
她	tā	she, her
他们	tāmen	they (male+female / male, pl.)
她们	tāmen	they (females, pl.)
这 (这儿)	zhè	here, this
那 (那儿)	nà (nàr)	there, that
哪 （哪儿）	nǎ (nǎr)	where
谁	shuí	who
什么	shén me	what, why
多少	duōshǎo	how many, how much
几	jǐ	a few, how many
怎么	zěnme	how
怎么样	zěnmeyàng	how about

Official MTHU Merch

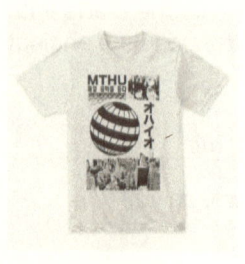

ハッピーdancing
Premium Tee
$16.99

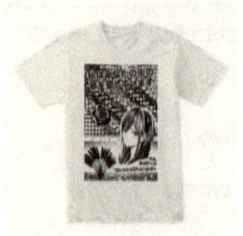

CityDream
Premium Tee
$16.99

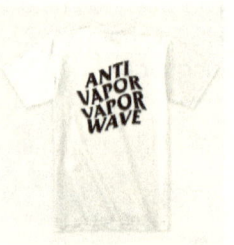

Anti Vapor Vaporwave on white
Premium Tee
$17.99

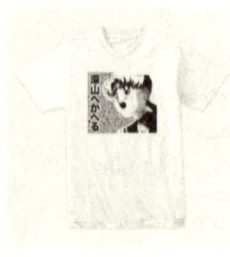

like flowers returning
Premium Tee
$16.99

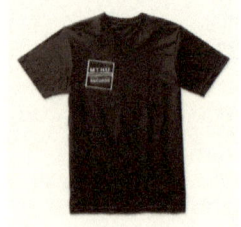

MTHU Records Class white
Premium Tee
$18.99

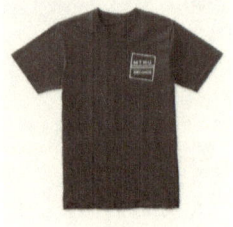

MTHU Records 2020 LOGO
Premium Tee
$18.99

Summer is finally here~ It's hot out, no need to hide your t-shirts under some hoodies, so let your body shine with some MTHU merch. Available now less than what you would pay for by any other vapor clothing line.

Grab some on Teespring!
https://teespring.com/stores/musics-the-hang-up

*Available in various colors and sizes

Outstanding Design Award

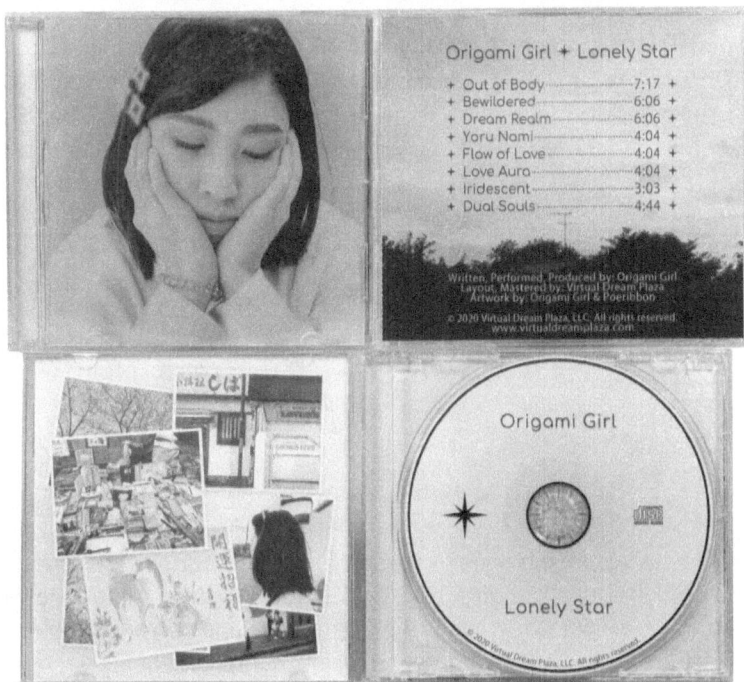

Origami Girl + Lonely Star

+ Out of Body ·········· 7:17 +
+ Bewildered ·········· 6:06 +
+ Dream Realm ·········· 6:06 +
+ Yoru Nami ·········· 4:04 +
+ Flow of Love ·········· 4:04 +
+ Love Aura ·········· 4:04 +
+ Iridescent ·········· 3:03 +
+ Dual Souls ·········· 4:44 +

Written, Performed, Produced by: Origami Girl
Layout, Mastered by: Virtual Dream Plaza
Artwork by: Origami Girl & Poeribbon

© 2020 Virtual Dream Plaza, LLC. All rights reserved
www.virtualdreamplaza.com

Origami Girl

Lonely Star

© 2020 Virtual Dream Plaza, LLC. All rights reserved

Lonely Star by Origami Girl

Released on May 8, 2020, Origami Girls latest bedroom dream pop album made it onto CD via Virtual Dream Plaza. The album cover was printed on a holographic sheet, so although the image above is in pink, it paints through the rainbow as you move the case around. Everything about this release screams emotional dusk aesthetics. I'm just hoping we see a cassette version with the same features. I want to own this kind of mood, I just don't have a CD player.

Recipient of the 1st MTHU Outstanding Design Award

Tsukemono Breakfast

In 2019, I had the opportunity to visit Japan with Sparkly Night, ADRIANWAVE & クリスタルKITSUNE. We all met up as they were invited to play Future Funk in Tokyo for the PITCH SHIFTER

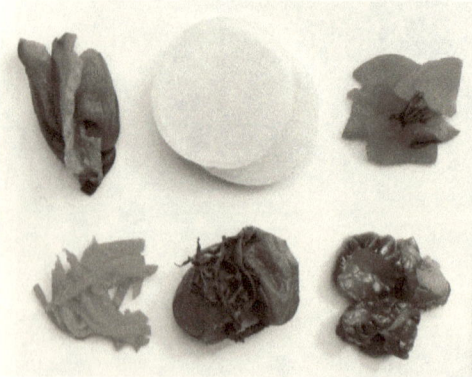

concert. It was a killer night, there's a recap of it on my YouTube channel, check it out.

Regardless of why I arrived in Tokyo, I did have a chance to wander the streets a few days earlier, alone. I stayed at a 12 USD a night hostel with 6 other dudes in the same room with me. I slept between a curtain between a young Japanese construction worker and another male I never had a chance to meet. Although, my head rested on a takamakura / 高枕 (a Japanese pillow) only a foot away from another dude, I slept better than I deserved. There's something magical about those beaded pillows. What a trip.

Every morning, the woman who ran the hostel would turn on a rice cooker and prepare breakfast for anyone who didn't mind waking up early. On a single tray she would arrange an assortment of tsukemono / 漬物 or pickled things. I say pickled things because I had no clue what this delicious food actual was but over the hot bowl of rice it made every morning a delicious treat.

A real Japanese memory I am nostalgic for. — KITE0080

C Y B E R I A **by kyonpalm**

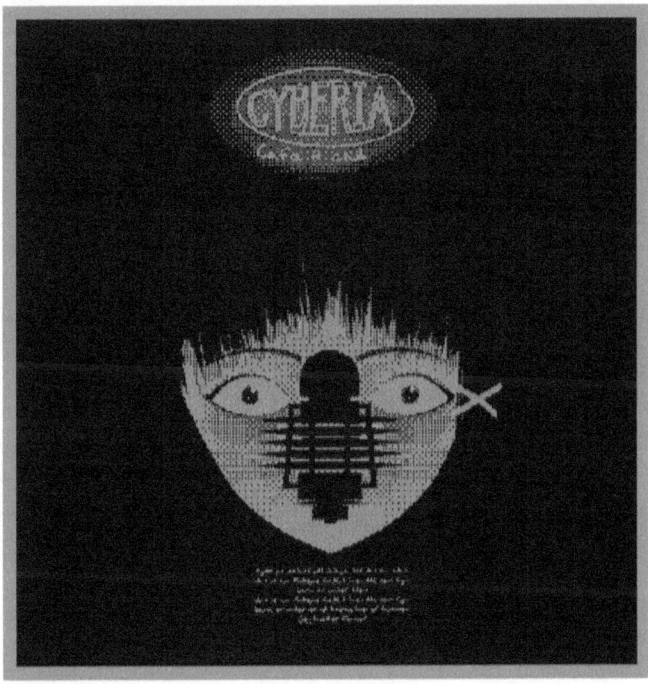

A classic from the early days of vapor, this funky "way better than It should be" release from 2014 still holds up in the new decade of vaporwave. When I first found this album in early 2019, it was the album art that original captured me. The solid black with minimal pink, outlining *Lain Iwakura* of *Serial Experiments Lain*, I knew the themes inside would hit that dark cyberpunk sound. The 13 track album had a handmade releases on cassette and a beautiful solid pink/red vinyl. Unfortunately, these were released before my time, which left my listening to the digital experience. I think this is were the love of collecting physical releases in our scene can spring up for a lot of fans because it's such a classic and unique release and yet we'll never get another physical copy. And even if I did want it, it's going for $100+ on Discogs. A+ album from the vault — KITE0080

Radio.garden APP ラジオ

FM Haro! 76.1	*Variety, Classic J-Pop and some American*	Hamamatsu, Japan
Mana'o Radio KMNO 91.7FM	*Variety*	Wailuku, Hawaii, USA
Ambient Sleeping Pill	*Just ambient music "for sleep, meditation or study; for tuning out distractions or simply relaxing"*	South Plainfield, New Jersey, USA
The Lot Radio	*Exclusively underground music*	New York City, New York, USA
99.9 JB.FM	*Adult Contemporary, Brazilian pop*	Rio de Janeiro, Brazil
*DUUU	*Experimental Electronic, and some variety*	Gennevilliers, France
Retro FM 88.3	*Classic Russian music from Funk, Pop, and Soul*	Moscow, Russia
Radio Nostalgie 101.1	*Retro favorites from the Ivory Coast!*	Abidjan, Côte d'Ivoire
Bondi Beach Radio	*Variety*	Bondi Beach, Australia
J1 Gold	*Classic Japanese music from the 60's - 90's*	Tokyo, Japan

Download the app at: http://radio.garden

June - August Weather reports

Average Temperature
June - August
Probability of below-normal temperature (cold), near-normal temperature (average), above-normal temperature (warm) for each area. Colored areas have a 40% probability or more of below-normal or above-normal temperature.

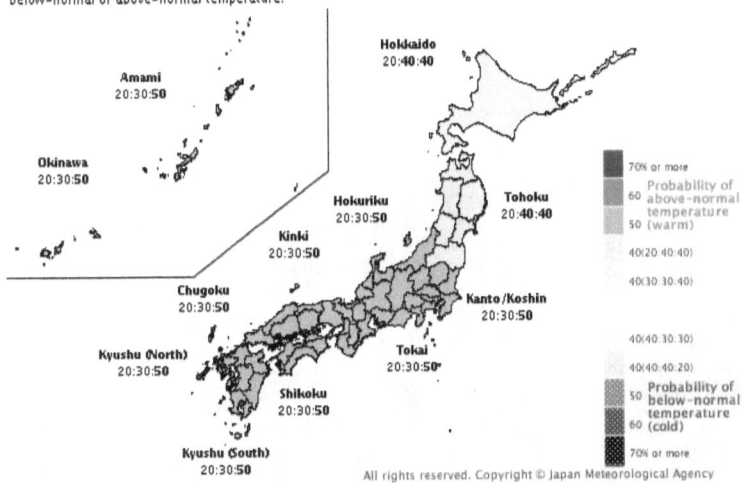

All rights reserved. Copyright © Japan Meteorological Agency

地図上をクリックすると各地方の詳しい予報がご覧いただけます。1か月予報は毎週木曜日14時30分、3か月予報は毎月25日頃14時、暖候期予報は2月、寒候期予報は9月の3か月予報と同時に発表します。このページの予報は、発表時刻から地方毎に順次更新されます。季節予報が発表された地方でも更新されるまでは前回発表の内容が表示されますので、季節予報の内容の確認は、1か月予報は14時40分以降、3か月予報・暖候期予報・寒候期予報は14時10分以降に全国の予報が完全に更新されてからお願いいたします。

One-month and three-month forecasts are issued at 14:30 JST every Thursday and at 14:00 JST around the 25th of each month respectively. Warm- and cold-season outlooks are issued in February and September respectively in concurrence with three-month forecasts.

围棋 (go) Full Game Kifu

Date : 2019-01-06
WhitePlayer : 围棋窗
WhiteRank : 17k
Komi : 6.5

BlackPlayer : KhengPohLim
BlackRank : 16k
Result : W+17.5

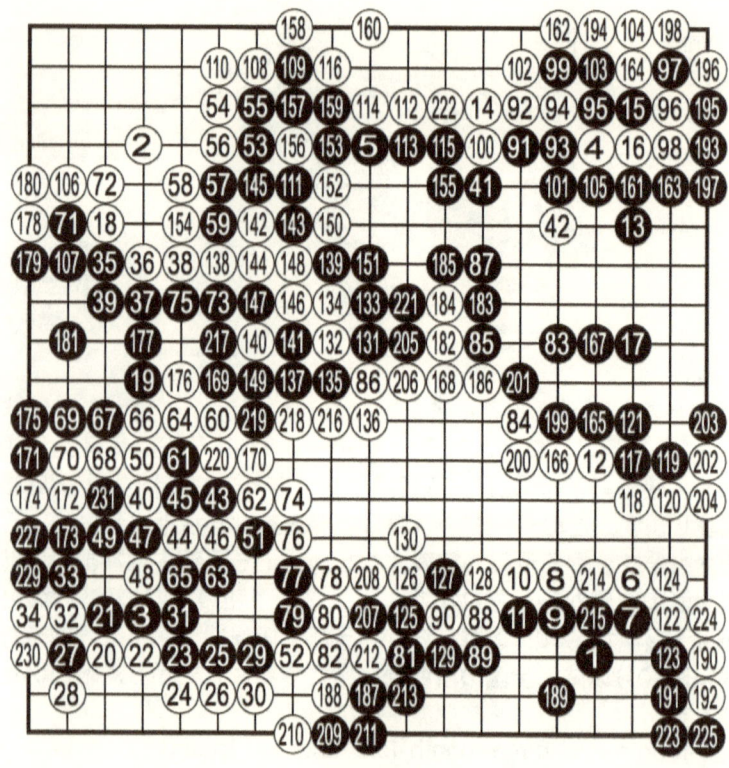

1 - 233

(228) at (226) (232) at (226)

パソコン音楽クラブ- reiji no machi

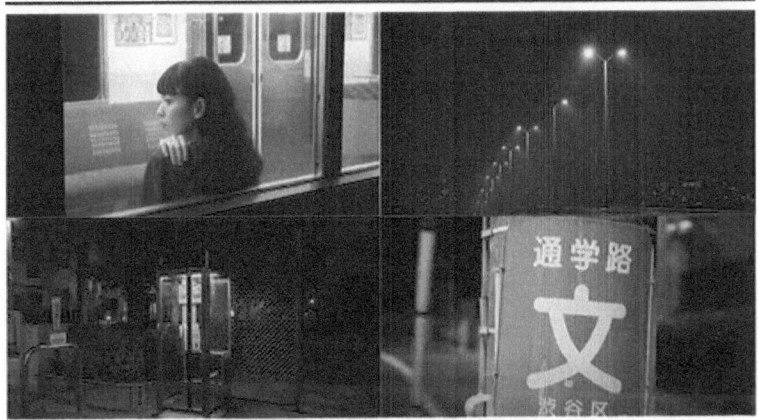

There's something special in finding a great song that takes your breath away because of the music video. The track *reiji no machi* by パソコン音楽クラブ from their second album 『Night Flow』 recently gave me one of the special moments. The tracks is rather poppy with a sad undertone but the synths keep it from feeling down but dramatic. The oddly peaceful females voice is keeps to the same 5 beat delivery until each hook. It works really well and is catchy even without understanding the Japanese.

On its own, the track is wonderful but the music video is what made it stand out for me. The director they hired, 田島太雄, takes these dramatic movements at fast and slow speed semi circles. This camera work applied to Japanese daily life, which makes it feel more special. What works so well is how clean and high quality the footage is while most scenes are dark. It's almost as if the use of lighting makes japan feel cleaner, brighter and almost artificial than it really is. So much so, that I wish my eyes could experienced life in this quality.

I just want to watch more footage like this, an entire movie if I could. It's addicting to see the world so perfect. — KITE0080

永远寻爱人

可说是一种衍生自亲人之间的强烈关爱、忠诚及善意的情感与心理状态，如母爱。亦可为衍生自性欲与情感上的吸引力，例如情人之间的情爱与温柔。此外，亦可能为衍生自尊敬与钦佩之情，例如朋友之间彼此重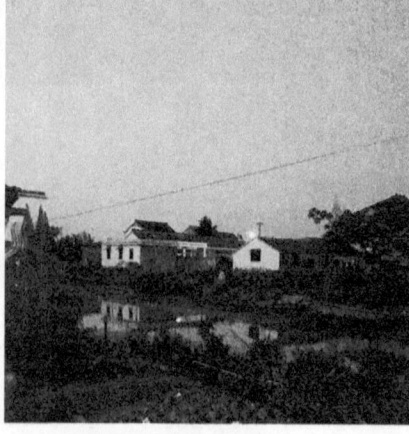视与欣赏。同时，爱被认为一种神奇的力量。爱，也可以是一个人的事。

心碎（英語：broken heart）是对一樣人、事、物有极大渴望卻求之不得，或是失去寶貴的人、事、物，在此之下感受到强烈情感（有时是身体的）压力或痛苦的隐喻。这个概念是跨文化的，经常被人用于指失恋，至少可以追溯到3000年前。严重的情感伤痛可导致"心碎综合征"，包括对心脏的伤害。

爱最佳的定义可能是主动行动，以真心对待某个生命体或物体（可以是人、动物、物品、神明），使其整体得到快乐。简而言之，爱即主动使整体得到快乐。 虽然世界各民族间的文化差异使得一个普世的爱的定义难以道明，但并非不可能成立（沙皮亚-沃尔福假设）。爱可以包括灵魂或心灵上的爱、对法律与组织的爱、对自己的爱、对食物的爱、对金钱的爱、对学习的爱、对权力的爱、对名誉的爱、对他人的爱等，数之不尽。为什么我没有爱人。爱人在哪？永远寻爱人。。。

山野·夏小虎

Latest MTHU Video

5 minutes of opening new cassettes

I had a couple of cassettes I haven't opened because I wanted to make individual videos for each. Instead I opened all of them in a short 5 minute video. Watch me even struggle to read 小圈子 by 輕描淡寫.

Top 100 Vaporwave Tracks

About 2 months ago, Pad Chennington asked wuso, Daydream Deluxe and myself to collaborate on a top 100 vaporwave tracks. We met up over Discord for about 3 weekends in a row, hung out and talk about vapor and built one of Pad's longest videos to date. It was awesome to work with the biggest names in the Youtube scene for Vaporwave and I hope everyone can enjoy the amazing animations Pad created to make our top 100s engaging. Which track do you think needs to be on the top 100? Let us know on the video.

Unboxing Retrospekt Cassettes

I recently bought and unboxed 2 indie cassettes off the team that revives retro tech. Check out Retrospekt if you're looking for refurbished cassette players, cameras or want new music on cassettes.

Zico's surprise!

I recently received a random package from Zico with two cassettes. One was a First Class Collective (Mr Wax) cassette and the other a special home-dubbed cassette of a certain MTHU Records release. Check out the video to find out which one!

Obviously, as of lately MTHU has turned into an unboxing channel. I hope to get more in person interviews going once I move to California, so look out for that in the future.

The Relevance of Liminal Space

Over the past few months, phrases like "Liminal Space" and "Places that feel oddly familiar and uncomfortable" has made its rounds over the internet. From subreddits to gimmick accounts on Twitter, Liminal Spaces has appeared in vast corners of the internet. So, why is it a talking point at the moment? Why is it important and is there something we can take from this term and the images it is often paired with?

Liminal Space means a space between one and another, like a hallway or a waiting room from comfort to a new normal. This space can be both visual or mental, from leaving the nest and going into college, to finding out your mom has cancer. We as humans learn from these thresholds to a new way of living. Threshold, is a key word for this topic; it means the magnitude or intensity that must be exceeded for a certain reaction, phenomenon, result, or condition to occur or be manifested. Threshold in Latin means "limen" which is the root word for our topic.

In photography, Liminal Space is trending with the aesthetics of emptiness, pastel wallpapers or flooring, grainy appearance, and dim lighting. It evokes feelings of anemoia, the nostalgia for a time you've never known. Or, even kenopsia, the eerie, forlorn atmosphere of a place that's usually bustling with people but is now abandoned and quiet. There is more to what meets the eye in these unsettling images, all art needs to be thoroughly digested.

As mentioned earlier, most of these images have similarities to the definition of Liminal Space. Many images follow the pattern of transition. From dark, empty rooms to long hallways that appear to have no ends or even a vacant big box store waiting to be bought by a new one. All of these locations have to do with change, and the lack of focus on any figure allows interpretation to be based on the person who sees it.

Liminal Space has become a movement. The setting we are living in and the entire world is transitioning dramatically resulting from the coronavirus pandemic. We as a society are evolving our life towards uncertainty, no one knows exactly what the future has for us, nor do we know how it will end up. But Liminal Space has a relatable outlet for all of us. It serves as a comforting reminder that we all go through change and sooner or later we will all get comfortable with our new normal. — MiddleClassComfort

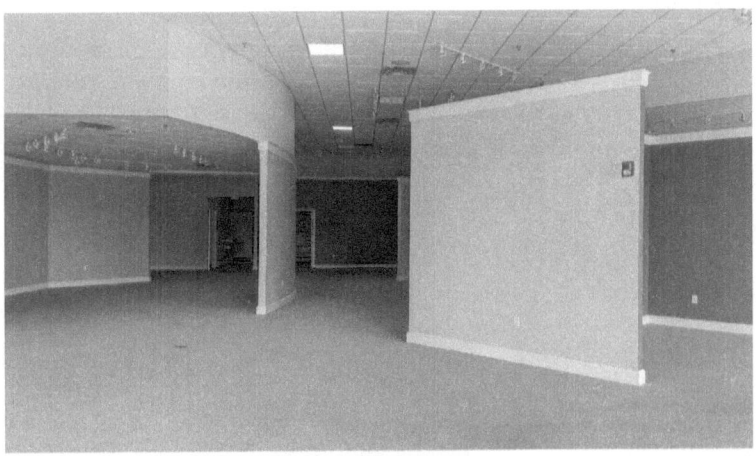

Fan Collection - Q

Vaporwave has found its ability to thrive in the digital world by allowing anyone to release music on any format. We've seen cassettes pop off since day one of the genre as Macintosh Plus' Floral Shop became the rarest cassette known in internet culture. Everyone wanted a piece of that lore and quickly cassette collecting in our scene became just as big as the genre itself. This issue we have Q sharing the top 5 from his collection.

100% Electronicon Mix Tape Volume 1

This tape will always hold a special place in my heart. Over a dozen signatures from artists and contributors to the scene, always kicks up memories of New York each time I listen. I met and made so many wonderful friends on that trip.

Future City Love Stories - Future City Love Stories

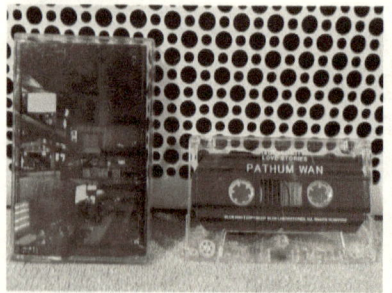

An underrated dreampunk classic, Pathum Wan contains beautifully airy synths soaked in rain. Yau Tsim Mong brings a busy and vibrant city drone. HKE has entangled feelings of love, angst, and curiosity into 45 minutes, both sides leaving you fully immersed in a smoky neon purple and red cityscape.

khoven - LSD: Pacificaの夢

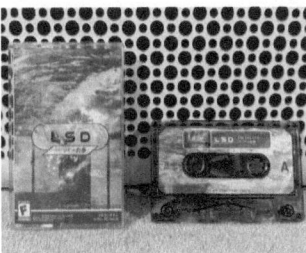

Guised as "Fish Simulation Software", khoven (AKA Valyri) has expertly woven drum n bass breaks flowing into serene trip hop beats. This album is such a fulfilling experience, leaves the listener in a state of bliss every time.

DJ Prom Knight - The Perfect Kiss

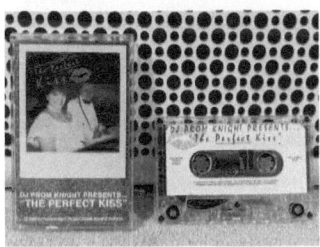

Another special tape for me, DJ Prom Knight (AKA Equip) has stepped into the slushwave ring with his first debut under this alias bringing us an album full of nostalgic prom memories. Each song gives off this energy that makes you yearn to experience that night once more.

CREEPS - Night Themes

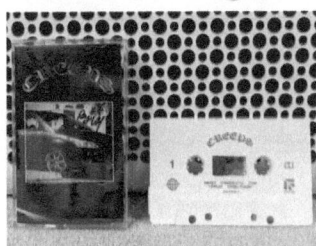

This is an album you'll have to sit down and hear for yourself. Rich, moody, and dark. Brings about feelings like you're in a noire film fifty years in the future. From Penny, one half of Surfing, this is like a sequel to Chrome.

Do you have an amazing cassette collection? Let us know @SignalsVisual on Twitter and we might feature your collections in the next issue!

The History of It All

Some of you might know I lived in Shenzhen, China for about 3 years. I had the opportunity to call it my home thanks to my previous job requesting me to go through an accelerator program. It was a trip of a life time and when my boss asked me if I'd like to stay, I said yes the second I had the chance. I loved living in the hotel across the street from the largest electronic market in the world (SEG Market). I was now being told I could get an apartment and live among the locals.

The first apartment I lived in was in 石厦. I had met my then girlfriend from being a cameraman on an indie featured film (check out my Sci-fi Novel "Limitations" by JD Riggs for my semi-biography as a cameraman) and she would end up moving in with me. I experienced the world because of her, but I was a fool and wanted more. I kicked her out like a ruthless and heartless man I was. I went down a spiral of misery and became depressed. I held up my job just fine but I felt like I would never be deserving my love again. I wish I never did the things I did to her back then. I wish I was still in her arms on these cold summer nights stuck in my hometown. Regardless, I had to move out of there.

I ended up finding, what would soon become, my favorite part of Shenzhen. 八卦岭, is where I became the man I am today. After reading more self-help posts about becoming my true self than I needed... I took up meditation and started scratching the creativity I had been suppressing. My first project was *Musics The Hang Up the podcast*. I started talking about music, mainly to make me feel less depressed. Then about some of the poets I loved. I was finding Jack Kerouac and Rod McKuen as ways to escape from my mind and take pride in the projects I was working. Art wasn't just something kids did. I just wasn't getting the audience I thought I would find. So I returned to my 2014 roots, the vaporwave scene.

Initially the podcast's biggest goal was to interview pop punk artists, with Title Fight being my biggest prize. The next best thing was the future funk and vaporwave artists I had been listening to in the past. So I reached out to a couple and all of a sudden the podcast about music turned into a podcast interviewing artists in our scene. As of this issue, I've interviewed 23 different people in the scene (Find them on bandcamp). I started musicsthehangup.com to start reporting on the scene and write reviews to hopefully get other artists noticed. I even started a calendar of releases (thanks Ethan) to get more people noticed.

The interviews were going great but no one was listening to them. So I started a YouTube channel. I wanted to do a podcast because I hated being in front of a camera. I was a cameraman on the indie film for a reason. Regardless, I started using simple editing software to make my interviews more interesting but still, I wasn't getting enough ears... So I did what Youtube was meant for, uploaded my face in a weekly news about Future Funk and Vaporwave and so it all began. I started uploading two YouTube videos a week and by the time I arrived at 100% Electronicon in New York, I had 100s of people coming up to me to talk. What surprised me with the whole stardom was, I didn't like how it made me feel. Like, I wanted so bad for people to watch my videos but I wanted to just do at least one creative project a week behind an alias. The attention was fun but not who I was, so I decided I was going to turn MTHU into documenting Future Funk and Vaporwave Concerts. In 2019, I went to 8 countries, saw 5 vapor concerts, met up with different people in the scene and put it all on YouTube for people to enjoy. Each one to this day are sub 1000 views.

Video after video of not getting views my rival (pad lol) had, I stopped making YouTube videos. My creative outlet was turning into shame and aggravation. So I just stuck to listening to music and talking to the scene on Twitter. Fortunately, I had the idea of making a book. I had been so into Signalwave that I wanted to add to the genre. I had yet to start making music at the time, so I did the next best thing; take images seen in 80s Japanese commercials and turn them into a visual experience. We all know it now as *A Book of Visual Signalwave* but at the time, no one had ever done anything like that. I still don't think any has really ever done anything like that. I didn't know what MTHU would look like in 2020, and I was starting to think the Signalwave book was going to be my big last project. But then I came home for Christmas and accidentally got stuck living at my fathers because of Covid. I had a lot of free time of my hands and so I started doing two things. Writing books (away from MTHU) and making music (starting MTHU Records).

I released a couple of EPs and then came out with ICいよてつど うJourney by メトロイヤー; "IYOTETSU or 伊予鉄道 is the main train provider in Matsuyama, Ehime, Shikoku, Japan. This album is a dedication to the sounds, the journey and the slice of life found on those railroad tracks." I didn't think too much of it but people actually really enjoyed the sound. I had wanted for a while to release a cassette and all things pointed this was the album to do it. I some how ended up selling 50 of them. I achieved a goal, make a cassette. Now I was left with no new goals for the vaporwave scene. I had maxed out on everything I ever wanted. I gave MTHU my all and I was seeing this isn't my life path…

So I wrote 6 books in 6 month under the made up publisher *3 Slashed Books*. I thought if I could just sell enough books a month, I could survive. I just wanted to survive. It wasn't working… so started getting down on myself again but I had a new tool; meditation. Every day I would say hundreds of 阿弥陀 佛s and ask the universe to please just give me the tools to survive. I need to survive. And it delivered, one morning on LinkedIn I get a message from a tech recruiter who put me through the rings of a couple of companies, leading me to get hired at a San Francisco based startup. It wasn't exactly what I was looking for, nor was it what I wanted but I took it was a sign. I was against the idea until my first day of work (Monday of this week funny enough) and everything seems to be working out. I am happy working again. I don't have any other choice, so I chose to give this job everything I have. I need to survive.

Ultimately, I started MTHU and all its projects with one hope; to live off my ability to be creative every single day and find worth in myself. I achieved that goal for a year and six months. I worked on a new project every single day, I made music, I wrote books, I created things that never existed. I was successful at making, I just couldn't figure out how to live off it. I am more than happy with my journey and the things I've shared with all of you. It lead to this one last project, the *Visual Signals: Issue Zero*.

I don't know what the future holds but I do hope I am able to make an *issue One*, Two and may more but I know I can't do that when I have given my creative mind to a company. I won't let the story end here, our future together will be long, just less output. Thank you for joining me, thank you for reading this, thank you for everything. I love all of you. Thank you for getting me this far and cheered me on along the way. Thank you MTHU for bringing me out of that depression and finding worth in who I am. Thank you China for giving me all the experiences that has led me to writing this note. Thank you universe and my mind for not giving up on me. Thank you.

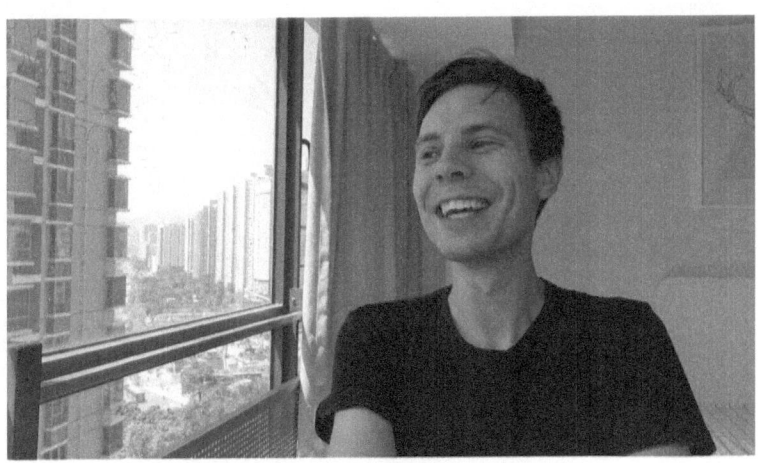

(above) me talking about Vaporwave
on camera in my 八卦岭 apartment

Issue Credits

All article / concepts / diagrams / ads / etc were developed by KITE0080 unless otherwise stated.

Note:
- Every artist, label, project, album, opinion, thought, tweet, post, blog, YouTube video, anything anyone posts is not my opinion. Every one of these things belong to the respective artist / label. I don't know what horrific thing someone might say in the future either. Don't hold me liable for it.

Credits:
- MiddleClassComfort (Ethan Adshead) // @MidClassComfy
    - Radio.garden APP ラジオ
    - The Relevance of Limited Space
- N3KKUN // @n3kkun
    - HATENA – Parader (Review)
- All cars found JDM auto were found on craigslist but are descriptions were fictional.
- SONY ICF-SW100 SW Radio images were found on a sold eBay listing
- Crossword generated at http://puzzlemaker.discoveryeducation.com/code/BuildCrissCross.asp
- Nobody Here Ad - Nobody Here design team
- Tsukemono Breakfast image (by Miki Kawasaki) https://www.seriouseats.com/2014/06/guide-japanese-pickles-tsukemono.html
- Ellie Sampson photos from their twitter @elliejsampson
- All logos / brands / album art belong to their respective owners

Contact KITE0080 // MTHU
- Twitter: @musicsthehangup // @SignalsVisual
- Instagram: @musicsthehangup
- Website: http://musicsthehangup.com
- Email: contact@musicsthehangup.com

Join the official MTHU Discord:
- http://musicsthehangup.com/discord

www.ingramcontent.com/pod-product-compliance
Lightning Source LLC
Chambersburg PA
CBHW030529220526
45463CB00007B/2766